SINCERELY YOURS, YOUR ONE TRUE LOVE

PURE LOVE SERIES

Denise Neal

AuthorHouse™
1663 Liberty Drive
Bloomington, IN 47403
www.authorhouse.com
Phone: 1 (800) 839-8640

ISBN: 978-1-7283-3098-3 (sc)
ISBN: 978-1-7283-3097-6 (e)

Print information available on the last page.

Published by AuthorHouse 10/08/2019

authorHOUSE®

SINCERELY YOURS,
YOUR ONE TRUE
LOVE

❦ *Dedication* ❦

Thank you father God for giving me the words I needed to express the love you have shown me and given me that I am now able to show and give, so that others can feel your love as well.

Brian Keith Carn Jr., you inspired me to push forth to continue to write these sweet words of encouragement and comfort, so that others could experience the pure love God has given us, so freely. Thank you for always allowing God to use you.

A love 🖤 so true

I will comfort you, when you needed me to. Because I love you! You are my love so true. So know your safe with me and when your feeling blue, I here with open arms to guide you safely through.
2 Cor. 1:3-5

A Part Of Me ❖

I know your name, I know your heart! You are apart of me, that's the way it was from the start. My love is never ending, there's no pretending; What I feel for you is real. My love can never be broken. Time and time again, it's been spoken.
Jeremiah1:5

Love shines in darkness ♥

In your dark days, I am here!
I will be the light you need to calm your fear. So when it seems I'm far always here, near to you; just a call away! Every moment of the day.
Genesis1:15

Pure Love

How wonderful you are!
In you I see no flaws. I love you with an everlasting love that descends upon you like a Dove.
I will keep you safe and warm, hide you from all harm. For you are my love, so whenever your in doubt just know! Your all I think about.
Jeremiah 29:11

Only 💍 You

I Just want you!
I want to be One with you.
I Just want to say, I love you
More than anything. Nothing
You can do or say, can change
The way I feel about you. I'm
Right here waiting for you, until
Your ready right say "I Do".
Jeremiah 3:14

Always Here ✿

I am here for you, my love.
All you have to do is call my
Name, without doubt or shame.
I will be your strength when you are weak, I will be there to encourage
you, when things look bleak. When fear Tries
To overtake you, just know!
I'm always here
Isaiah 41:10

All Mine! ❀

You are wonderful in my sight,
You are created just like just for me. I don't want to share you with
anyone else, I want you all
To myself. My love is pure, you never have to doubt! because
My love is sure.
Exodus 34:14

Love 🌹 Never Fades

My love, you can count on me!
Because I will never leave.You
Are mine and I am yours, from
Sea to Sea, to the distant shores! My love for you soars.
Hebrews 13:5

Me Without You

1 isn't my favorite number because it means me, without
You, like a mountain without a view, like sky without the color
Blue, me without you! Just won't do.
John 15:4-5

Forever Love

I know your heart, my love
Shall never part. I loved you
From the beginning, I love now!
My love is never ending, I will love you for all eternity; and just
Know! You will always be apart of me.
Jeremiah 31:3

One Of A Kind

Today is like unto a new song,
With the sweetest melodies never sang before. It is as precious as you
are to me, Never to be taken for granted!
and always a blessing.
Lamentations 3:22-23

Love Beyond Words

I am honored every day,
When you take the time
To communicate with me.
As I said before, our love
was meant to be. My love
For you! I will always show,
How deep it goes; you will
Never know.
Job 22:27

Patiently Waiting

I Miss you when I don't hear
From you, I'm right here!
Waiting for you. It doesn't take
Much, for your voice is such a sweet sound in my ear, you
Should know by now! my love
For you is sincere.
Matthew 7:7-11

Eye Of The Beholder

How beautiful you are to me,
Like the fresh bloom of spring.
Your like no other, I won't fine another like you. When I'm with
You everything in my world is
Brand new.
2 Corinthians 5:17

Real Love

This is not a fairytale, a love so true! one in which I'm happy to say I
invested all in you.
John 3:16

Safe Haven

Heaven is my home with you, no place else will do. you're where my heart is, my heart lies with you. no one else can take your place, with me you'll always be safe.
John 14:3

Unbreakable Love

My love, my world we share!
This love we have, no one can tear it apart. There's a reason for our Union, it's Way Beyond human knowledge. Soon, the love we share! Everyone will acknowledge.
Proverbs 3:3-4

Amazing Love

There's newness in the air,
I can feel it ever so near. So I dance new dance with you, so Carefree! without you, I could never be. I don't have to worry, our love tells the story! Of a love so amazing and true.
Isaiah 43:18-19

Oneness

Before you think of me I'm there! one heart, one mind we both share. What a beautiful connection, you're my reflection. this is a love so deep, no one else can compete.

John 4:16

My Heartbeat

The Light Within Me shines brighter Because You Love Me.

It can't be hidden under a bush or any kind of tree, the love you have for me is amazing. It burns brighter than the Morning Light so, in I heart your love I keep, with every heartbeat.

Matthew 5:16

Indescribable Love

What I feel for you, words cannot describe. Love overflowing inside, bursting through the seams, a love I cannot hide. Like a tidal wave that cannot be controlled, so big and bold! Like a story that cannot wait to be told.
2 Corinthians 9:15

Never Part

You are wonderfully made for me, not a dream but I love that can clearly be seen. You're my king and I your queen, together as one even after this life is done.
John 10:28

Love shining through

The sun shines brightly through, even when my skies are gray; because of you. You're always here for me, now there's nothing I can't do because you give me the strength to.
Philippians 4:13

Unblinding Love

Ever since I met you! my life has never been the same. You are the miracle I needed, even when I couldn't see it.
John 9:25

Sure Love

A day anew, another chance to be with you. Never thought I'd find a love so true but I found it in you.
1 John 4:10-12

Unknowing Love

Your thoughts towards me! created my future, even when I didn't know much about you, you still love me and brought me through.
Jeremiah 29:11

Love So Deep

In the beginning was a fight, but now! I can't let you out of my sight. You turn my dark days bright, make me want to go deeper depths and higher Heights.
Deuteronomy 7:9

Love Knows No Limits

Because of you, I dream dreams and never thought possible, no obstacle can stand in my way. whatever I say! it will happen, no longer a ship without Direction.
Proverbs 18:21

Destined ❤ Love

I always belonged to you and never even knew, you're my love so true. A dream come true, that's when I knew! you and me will never part no matter what we do.

Deuteronomy 31:6

Eternal Love 🖤

You are real! you're my love, I feel it each and everyday; what else can I say. We went our separate ways but found our way back to each other, from this day forth! there will never be another.

Jeremiah 3:14

Undoubting Love 🌹

We were meant before the foundation of the world, like tiny grains of sand, it was all in God's plan. there is no doubt it's you I can't live without.

Jeremiah 29:11

Kiss Of Love

My world is better with you, a love like this I never knew. it's like a sweet kiss every morning! the kind you don't want to miss. My world with you! this is it, anything else just won't fit.
Matthew 19:26

Love's Reality

I never knew true love exists, it always felt like a myth. Ever since you found me, I come to realize! things that was once out of reach, can now be. I see things in a new light, with new sight.
Romans 12:2

Language Of Love

There's no words to describe the love I feel for you, all the words in the dictionary just won't do. so for now! I will use what I have. You make my soul glad because of you I'm no longer sad.
Isaiah 61:1-3

Beyond Expectations

You and me fit together like a hand in a glove, the love we share comes from above. no limits, no boundaries with this love I'm able to see, not what would have been but what could be.
Ephesians 3:20-21

Sweet Eternity

Your love is like a gentle sweet spring Breeze, so lovely and sweet as a summer Peach. A love always and forever, a love that can't be severed.
Psalm 119:103

New Found Strength

Your love has given me the strength to get through anything. I know you want the best for me, through your love I can clearly see; what I can be. now, my life's renewed because of you.
2 Corinthians 5:7

Love Beyond Reason

You have opened my eyes to see, what I could not see before; or what I choose to ignore. Because you loved me, all things are possible. Now I'm unstoppable, so thank you for your love, for this love can only come from above.
Isaiah 35:5

Eternal Love

You pour your love upon me, like a sweet perfume. If Loving You Is Wrong! then I'll be the fool. eternal love is what I'm speaking of. There's no love like this, eternal Bliss!
2 Corinthians 2:15

Now And Forever!

You are the light of my life, I'm so blessed to know you! we are now part of each other, that's the way it's meant to be. It's always been you and me.
1 Corinthians 6:17

A Love Beyond Time

Your love covers me, like the waters that cover the ocean floor. I opened the door and let you in, I feel a Love never felt before, a love that flows from the Seas to Distant Shores. I am yours.
1 Peter 4:8

Love Overflowing

Your love is peace, your love is Joy, your love calms my spirit, it makes me soar. I have no worries in you, because your love is true.
James 1:2-3

Forever And Always

Even in my darkest days, your love shines bright to show me the way. so I say thank you for loving me in such an unconditional way, here is where I want to stay! Close to you, don't ever go away.
Proverbs 6:23

Unsure 🌸

When I'm in a place of uncertainty, knowing you love me give me Clarity. Because I know you love me with all sincerity, with you is where I want to be.
Romans 5:5-11

Purposed love 🌹

My love for you is without a doubt, it is you I can't live without. There's a purpose, there's a plan! it's all in his hands. I won't try to figure it out or find out what is all about, because you have it covered! My one true lover.
John 10:10

Unfamiliar territory 🌸

I've never been here before, but yet I have! you make me laugh when I'm feeling sad. you're all I need, I will go wherever you lead.
Romans 8:14

Dreams ❤ Of Love

Your Love shines down on me like rays of sunshine, warms my soul with riches Untold. Your love captivates me, makes me want to see Beyond Hills and Valleys and dream dreams, never dreamt before. thank you for opening that door.
2 Corinthians 4:6

Love Anew/Pure And True 🌹

Love with you is pure and true. like a new song everyday! that I want to play over and over again, without end. Your the song that lifts my soul, your the story that cannot wait to be told. I love you always and forever, for this love could never be severed.
1 Timothy 1:14-16

Captive Love 🌹

I've been captured by a love I can't explain, and now you have me! I'm forever changed. No more guilt or shame you carry my pain, nothing will ever be the same.
Galatians 6:17

Always Yours ❀

Starting over with you, a life brand new. A chance to right wrongs, with you is where I belong always and forever.
2 Corinthians 5:17

Light Of Love 💝

Like a miracle, you came into my life. Something I can't figure out but it doesn't even matter because I can't let you go, to you I hold tight. My soul burns bright! with the light of Your Love.
John 6:51

Flowing Love 🌹

Your love is something I can't live without, it makes me want to shout from the rooftops. Like a river that flows freely; I never wanted to stop.
John 7:38

Direction 🌸

My life always flowed in the direction of you, even with the detours and hinderance too. the love you have for me! I never even knew, before the beginning of time we were meant to be.
Proverbs 3:5-6

No Longer A Dream 🌸

Who would have known that a dream would turn into reality, I couldn't see that it was always you and me. The impossible is now possible because now I believe.
Psalm 37:4

Patiently Waiting 🌸

A love that words can describe! a great time to be alive! love showered down on me, even in times couldn't feel it. It was there waiting for me to receive it, so patiently and calm until the appointed time.
2 Peter 3:9

Wanted Love 🌹

You are my everything! you make my heart sing, I don't want for anything because I have you.You pursued me and gave me love, you made me want to know you! even in times I never even wanted to, and so, I Thank you.
Matthew 6:31-32

Love Story 🖤

Glory Glory Glory! let me tell the story of a love that began before the beginning of time a love That's truly mine. A love I thought I'd never find.
1 Corinthians 13

Paradise

It amazes me every day. I'm so glad to say; you are my lover, my friend! you will be with me, for all eternity. When I spend time with you, I feel a love I never knew.
Joshua 1:5

A Great Love

A love I can't explain! I know this might sound lame, but I feel a pain in my heart whenever you're not with me or so it seems. A love not only one can bear but together it feels like floating on feathers.
Matthew 11:28-30

Perfectly You

If I could create the perfect man, It would be you! there's nothing I would change! nothing I would do; because just the way you are! perfectly suits.
Psalm 18:30

A Better Me ❀

What can I do for you? what dream can I make come true? that's what you say to me, when you love me the way you do. You send angels to earth! to help and guide me when I feel low self-worth.

Isaiah 40:31

Love 🌹

We have a love so lovely! a love so pure, a love unexplainable, a love to hold dear. A once-in-a-lifetime love that can only come from above.

Ephesians 4:2

One

You pull things out of me, things I never knew I could ever be. you've now become a part of me; you are my breath when I can't breathe, my eyes when I can't see. we are one now, for all eternity.
1 John 4:13

Destined

My life has changed because of you! even with all I've been through, it all led right back to you. Promise kept! even when I wasn't aware, a life with you I'll always share.
Romans 5:8

Love ❤ From Heaven

You are beyond my wildest imagination! Like a vacation I never thought I could have. Our love is made to last, a love I never thought would come to pass.
Jeremiah 31:3

No Love Like Mine 🌹

I am your heartbeat, you are mine. it's been that way since the beginning of time! together we shine, a love like ours; you'll never find. Because just like us! it's one of a kind.
Zephaniah 3:17

Love's Destiny ❤

To be? or not to be? there is no question! you have truly been a blessing. My angel, my miracle! I couldn't ask for anyone better. Like two birds of a feather, We Belong Together.
Psalm 36:7

Created Love 🌹

I was created for you! with a future I never knew. You and me together, a love so true. A destiny only you knew! so I just want to say thank you.
Habakkuk 2:3

In 💗 Love

Everyday with you is amazing! there's no Aging in the love we share. It is so pure and innocent, like a cool swimming pool! in the Blazing summer heat. I want to stay in it, I always want to love you.
John 16:33

Sincerely Yours 💋

Sincerely yours, from here! to distance shores. From the surface to the ocean floor, I love you to the core. No need to say anymore.
Romans 8:38-39

Love, Love, Love 🖤

There's no words to cover how I feel about you. You are my love so true. From the highest mountain, to the ocean blue! I want the whole world to know oh! how I love you.
John 3:16

Don't Need A Star ✦

I don't need a star to wish upon every night, thoughts of you keep me warm and holds me tight. I don't need a star to wish upon every night, because you're my star in my darkest nights. I don't need a star to Wish Upon every night, because all my dreams came true! when I met you.
John 8:12

Free

I will never be bound again! I got my Liberty, I'm finally free. Free to dream, free to love, free to live. In you there will never be another so true; I desire Only You.
John 8:36

I Belong To You

There is no other to be compared to you, you are my one and only.There will never be another that will take your place, for you make my space better.
1 John 4:4

Forever Love

Forever love! is what we are. Forever love, from the start. Forever love will never part. you're my dream come true, always and forever.

Unconditional

A love so faithful and true! all I want is you.You always want to take care of me; no matter what I do. Your love is so unconditional, a love I thought I never find; but I'm so glad to say! you're all mine.

Kept Promise

A promise made, never to be broken. A sweet word fitly spoken. You calm my spirit whenever it's needed. With your love I'm Victorious! never defeated.

A Brighter Day 🌸

My days were filled with dark clouds, even when the sun was out! you came and changed my darkness into day, you are now in my heart to stay. And I know now! that everything will be okay.
Isaiah 41:10

Only You 🌸

What should I say! at the beginning of a beautiful day, thoughts of you filll my heart; love overflowing, it's a great feeling to a wonderful start. You're my one and only! no one else but you will ever do.
Deuteronomy 4:35,39

Love Agape 🌹

You never break I promise! you always leave me astonished at things you do for me, even the things I cannot see. I can always count on you to be forever true. You will never let me down. You are always around, whenever I need you. when I'm feeling blue, when I'm feeling happy, even when I don't know how I feel! you're still there, showing me how much you care.
2 Corinthians 12:9-10

Speechless 🌹

I know your deepest thoughts and most intimate feelings, you don't have to speak a word. I know what to do for you! when your skies are gray and you're feeling blue, you don't have to speak a word,! I am your one true love And We Are One.
Romans 8:27-29

Forever True 💗

Forever is a long time! but that's how long I'll love you, that's how long I'll love you, forever! This is my promise to you.
forever true.
1 John 4:16

Love's Journey 💕

Your love for me has stood the test of time. It fills my heart with joy and makes me want to shine. You're so patient and kind! this kind of love is hard to find. Traveling through generations, Soul and Spirit together! not by force but because we were destined.
Psalm 119:90

Sweet Melody 🌸

Your love is the sweetest Melody that keeps my heart beating every day! It's the only song that makes me want to sing along. It's like a breath of fresh air! that last forever, in a world that doesn't care. Without your love I have no reason to Breathe.
Psalm 19:10

Unexplainable 🌹 love

Pure love with no strings attached, this is what I found in you. A love I never knew until I found you.The thought of you makes me want to love more than I ever thought possible. you love me past my crazy, your love takes me places I never thought I'd go. Unconditional love is what you always show.
Psalm 103

Sight Unseen 🌸

You give me the strength I need to keep going with you, even with my ups and downs your love remain true. You give my life new meaning every morning. Because of you,! I now see. I can truly say, I am free and can receive, all that you have for me.
Proverbs 10

The One 🌸

You are warm, you are kind, you are patient, you are one in a million 2nd To None. You are the one. You found me when I had no hope, when I thought I couldn't cope. You brought life back into my spirit! now I can feel you ever so near. You're never going to leave me, you make me believe again!
Isaiah 40:31

Love Without A reason 🌹

I love you because I love you. there's no Rhyme or Reason or any season for that matter! That caused love to shine so strongly upon you, and to know you love me too! it's a dream come true. My whole world changed, the day I said I do.
John 15:13

Unseen 💖

I see you everyday in the little things you do for me.
So even though you're not here physically! you're right by my side loving and guiding me, in times when I'm I'm sure; You are there to restore. Thank you for all the things you do and even though I can't see you, you are there!
1 Peter 1:8-9

Eternal Sunshine 🌸

Everyday with you is like an eternity of sunshine shining down on me
Your Love warms me up when things are cold and I begin to feel numb inside
and it brightens my spirits when things are dark my soul is eternally grateful
to know that you will never leave my side.
Psalm 94:19

Deeper 🌸

My love for you is deep! deeper than the deep blue sea,
longer than the East is from the West, higher than the stars and the
moon. No eye can see, no height can measure! the love I have for you. There
is no end in sight.
Lamentations 3:22-24

No Grey Skies 🌸

No situation I face, is too great for you. Gripping tightly to your love, I know there is nothing I can't get through. I'm always assured, with you by my side; the love that we share Has the strength to always abide.
Psalm 23

Always 🌸

The love we share, can't be compared to any other. You never have to worry! if my love is true because me, not loving you; is impossible.
Psalm 136:1-26

Sweet ♥ Love

Your love is sweeter than the honey on a honeycomb. refreshing as a sweet juicy watermelon on a hot summer's day, as inviting as a cool breeze on a warm spring Eve. You wrap me up in your love, like a warm blanket on a cold Winter's Night. It keeps me safe and holds me tight.
Psalm 34:8

A Dream 💕

You love me so much! even when my world is crazy, you don't blame me. You cover me with patience and kindness, sometimes it feels like a dream. it makes me wonder if this is reality, but you keep telling me yes! it's true, I love you; I really do. And it shows in everything you do for me.
John 4:19

Oh! How you Love Me 💖

You love me and give me strength, you protect me from all hurt and danger. All my anger disappears and all that's left, is happy tears. You make me feel a way I thought I never could, you teach me to love the way I should.
Psalm 1-3

Because of your love ♥

Because of your love my story has changed. Now a story worth telling, the time has come! all the yelling in my head has ceased and finally I have peace. Because of your love, I have a story to tell now me came we. No longer alone but deep in love, a resting place! a place called home. Because of your love!
Isaiah 43:18-19

You 🌹

You are my sunrise, in my dark and cloudy skies. Everything is brighter because of you, you make everything in my world okay, you're so amazing! I can't find the words to say. You're always there when I don't expect you to be; but then I remember! you promised you would always be.
Isaiah 43:1

Adoring Love 🌹

Because of you, I now know what true love is. No longer have to settle for less, because you bring the best out of me. Your all I could ever ask for, your the one I adore.
Mark 12:30

Because You Love Me ❤

There are no words to explain the peace I feel, because you I love me. Knowing I can do anything! because you love me. there's no limits, only possibilities, Because You Love Me.
Philippians 4:13

Time With You 💖

I smile like the sunshine; on my face, from day-to-day. Anticipating the time I get to spend with you. Holding tight to every moment! never wanting it to end.
Psalms 5:3

Yes ❀

You pushed me past my greatest potential, you said you would be all I needed you to be. I'm always at a loss for words when it comes to you. sometimes I feel your too good to be true.Is this real! the love you feel; for me. Can this be the love I've searched for, for so long! and the answer is yes!
Jeremiah 29:11

Patient Love Kind Love ❀

Love is patient, love is kind! it's not only said but it's deep on the inside of you. I hear it when you speak to me, I see it in your eyes and I feel it all the time. love is patient, love is kind it's not just a word you say but it's what you live by. Your forever true to me! I can clearly see that you love me.
1 Corinthians 13:4-8

Without You 💖

Without you! I'm broken like half of a whole. Without you I'm lost, like a ship In a storm! with no hand to hold; because you calm my seas and now I'm able to breathe.
Colossians 2:10

What Is Love 🌹

Love is one word! but it's much more than that. It can't be described and it won't fit in the Box. Love is free to flow where it must and changes the hearts of everyone who it touches; by it's warm embrace, you that know it's presence keeps you safe.

Psalm 91

You Still Love Me 💖

You still love me even when I can't see it, you still love me. Even when I can't feel it, you still love me. You still love me, even when I didn't know it, even when I fail to believe! you still love me.

Jeremiah 31:3

Love's Touch 🌹

Your love for me was meant to be. I never imagined that someone could love me this much! I longed for the day to feel your touch. long-awaited much imagine, you and me together finally!

Titus 3:4-5

In The Presence Of Love 💋

Being in your presence is all I long for. My torn heart is whole again, because of you. Being without you just won't do. You told me I was precious to you! I know your love for me is true; because of the things you do.
Psalm 16:11

Always There 🌹

You are the most loving I know. ever so kind, ever so patient. You exceeded All my expectations, with you I never have to worry, never have to be afraid! you always make sure I'm safe.
Isaiah 41:10

Half Of A Whole 💗

There's no me without you, We are part of each other! two halves of a whole. two becoming one.
Romans 4:10

Holding On ❀

Your love is so strong! it holds onto me, even when I want to let go. When it feels like; what's the point! when it feels like; it's not even worth it! love is there to say; I'm here for you, in every single way. So when you feel like giving up and you want to throw in the towel, take a step back and remember! In that hour; love is there to carry you through. A love so great, a love so true.

1 John 4:19

Strength In Love ❀

I got to be strong, because I'm right where I belong; with you. I've been waiting so long for someone like you, someone I never knew existed. But your love persisted to keep me holding on, while showing me we belong together.

2 Corinthians 12:9

Breathe ❀

One hour is too long to be without you, let alone days! because that feels an eternity. Being without you; is like being in a room without windows or doors no way to escape! nothing to hope for. Having you in my life gives me the courage I need and the strength to fight.
John 15:5

Perfection ❀

The light of your love, descends upon me like a dove. It brings an end to my dark nights, a light that never goes out! can't tell you what it's all about a light so pure, a love so perfect; the kind of love that comes from above.
Number 6:25

Printed in the United States
By Bookmasters